Letts and Lonsdale

GCSE Success

Workbook

AQA Physics

How to Use this Workbook

This workbook has been written and developed to be used alongside the revision guide, **AQA GCSE Physics Success**, to help you get the most out of your revision. You can use it if you are studying AQA GCSE Physics Foundation or Higher Tier.

It contains 'quick fire' questions, including multiple choice questions, matching pair exercises and short answer questions, to test your understanding of the topics covered in the revision guide.

Start by reading through a topic in the revision guide. Make notes, jotting down anything that you think will help you to remember the information. When you have finished, take a short break and then read through your notes. You might even want to try covering them up and writing them out again from memory.

Finally, work through the relevant questions in this workbook without looking at the guide or your notes.

The page headers and sub-headings in this workbook correspond with those in your revision guide, so that you can easily identify the questions that relate to each topic.

Completing the questions will help to reinforce your understanding of the topic covered in the guide and highlight any areas that need further revision.

The answers to the questions in this workbook are available in a separate booklet. There is a box at the end of each page for you to record your score. Don't worry if you get some questions wrong the first time. Just re-read the information in your revision guide and try again.

The tick boxes on the contents page let you track your revision progress: just put a tick in the box next to each topic when you're confident that you understand it.

Good luck with your exams!

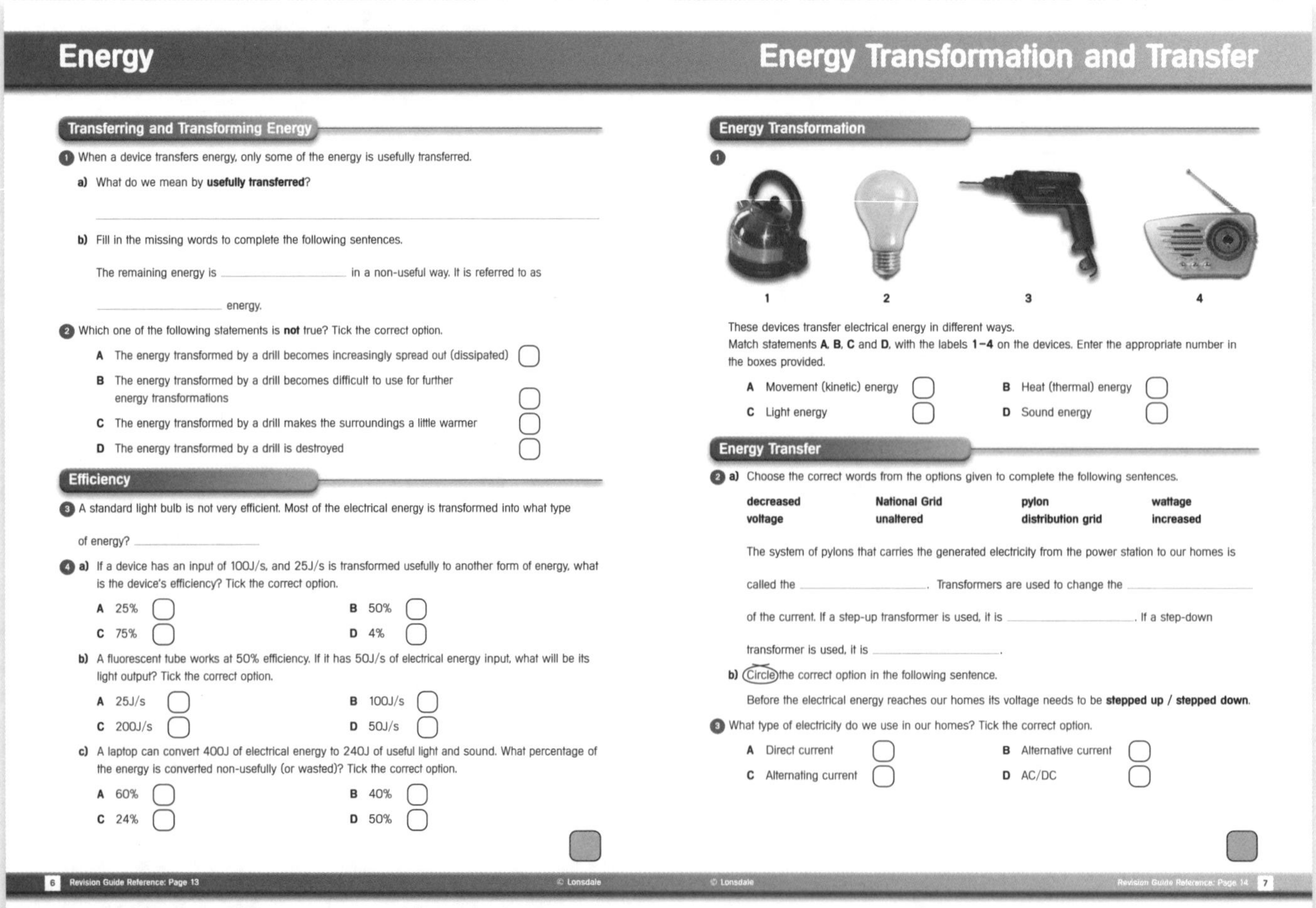

Energy

Transferring and Transforming Energy

1. When a device transfers energy, only some of the energy is usefully transferred.
   a) What do we mean by **usefully transferred**?
   b) Fill in the missing words to complete the following sentences.
   The remaining energy is ______ in a non-useful way. It is referred to as ______ energy.
2. Which one of the following statements is **not** true? Tick the correct option.
   A The energy transformed by a drill becomes increasingly spread out (dissipated)
   B The energy transformed by a drill becomes difficult to use for further energy transformations
   C The energy transformed by a drill makes the surroundings a little warmer
   D The energy transformed by a drill is destroyed

Efficiency

3. A standard light bulb is not very efficient. Most of the electrical energy is transformed into what type of energy? ______
4. a) If a device has an input of 100J/s, and 25J/s is transformed usefully to another form of energy, what is the device's efficiency? Tick the correct option.
   A 25% B 50% C 75% D 4%
   b) A fluorescent tube works at 50% efficiency. If it has 50J/s of electrical energy input, what will be its light output? Tick the correct option.
   A 25J/s B 100J/s C 200J/s D 50J/s
   c) A laptop can convert 400J of electrical energy to 240J of useful light and sound. What percentage of the energy is converted non-usefully (or wasted)? Tick the correct option.
   A 60% B 40% C 24% D 50%

6 Revision Guide Reference: Page 13 © Lonsdale

Energy Transformation and Transfer

Energy Transformation

1. 1 2 3 4
   These devices transfer electrical energy in different ways.
   Match statements **A**, **B**, **C** and **D**, with the labels **1–4** on the devices. Enter the appropriate number in the boxes provided.
   A Movement (kinetic) energy B Heat (thermal) energy
   C Light energy D Sound energy

Energy Transfer

2. a) Choose the correct words from the options given to complete the following sentences.
   decreased **National Grid** **pylon** **wattage** **voltage** **unaltered** **distribution grid** **increased**
   The system of pylons that carries the generated electricity from the power station to our homes is called the ______. Transformers are used to change the ______ of the current. If a step-up transformer is used, it is ______. If a step-down transformer is used, it is ______.
   b) Circle the correct option in the following sentence.
   Before the electrical energy reaches our homes its voltage needs to be **stepped up / stepped down**.
3. What type of electricity do we use in our homes? Tick the correct option.
   A Direct current B Alternative current
   C Alternating current D AC/DC

© Lonsdale Revision Guide Reference: Page 14 7

Contents

Unit 1a

Unit 1b

Unit 2

Unit 3

Conduction, Convection and Radiation

Conduction and Convection

1 Circle the correct options in the following sentences.

a) **Conduction / convection** is the transfer of heat energy through the movement of a substance.

b) **Conduction / convection** is the transfer of heat energy through a substance without the substance itself moving.

2 Fill in the missing words to complete the following sentences.

a) The process of heat energy being transferred along a metal bar is called ....

b) The process of heat energy being transferred through a liquid is called ....

c) The process of heat energy being transferred through a gas is called ....

3 Which of these statements about metals is **not** true? Tick the correct option.

A Metals are good conductors because they contain free electrons that are able to move through the metal ☐

B Metals are good conductors because they do not have free electrons that are able to move through the metal ☐

C As the metal becomes hotter, its particles gain more kinetic energy ☐

D As the metal becomes hotter, the free electrons move faster ☐

4 a) Soup is cooked in a metal saucepan on a camp fire. How is the thermal energy transferred through the metal of the saucepan? Tick the correct option.

A By free electrons colliding with particles and other electrons ☐

B By the atoms moving faster through the metal ☐

C By infra red radiation moving through the metal ☐

D By the heated metal expanding, becoming less dense and rising ☐

b) How does the thermal energy spread through the soup? Tick the correct option.

A By hot air rising ☐

B By the soup expanding, becoming less dense and rising ☐

C By the soup contracting, becoming denser as it is heated ☐

D By free electrons colliding with atoms ☐

5 Circle the correct option in the following sentence.

A radiator heats the air in a room by **radiation / convection / conduction**.

Conduction, Convection and Radiation

Radiation

1 Fill in the missing words to complete the sentence below.

Infra red radiation is the transfer of heat energy by ....

2 How is the transfer of heat by infra red radiation different from the transfer of heat by conduction or convection?

....

3 **a)** Which of the following statements about the emission and absorption of infra red radiation are true? Tick the **two** correct options.

- **A** Black is a good absorber and emitter ☐
- **B** Black is a poor absorber and emitter ☐
- **C** Black is a poor absorber and good emitter ☐
- **D** Black is a good absorber and poor emitter ☐
- **E** Light, shiny materials are good absorbers and emitters ☐
- **F** Light, shiny materials are poor absorbers and emitters ☐
- **G** Light, shiny materials are poor absorbers and good emitters ☐
- **H** Light, shiny materials are good absorbers and poor emitters ☐

b) Which of the following statements about infra red radiation are true? Tick the **three** correct options.

- **A** All objects emit and absorb thermal radiation ☐
- **B** The cooler the object, the more energy it radiates ☐
- **C** The amount of radiation an object gives out or takes in depends on its surface ☐
- **D** The amount of radiation an object gives out or takes in depends on its shape and dimensions ☐

4 Circle the correct option in the following sentence.

An object will emit or absorb energy **faster / slower** if there's a big difference in temperature between it and its surroundings.

5 Samuel has a glass jug of very hot liquid. How would you suggest...

a) he can slow down the rate at which it emits heat to keep it hotter for longer?

....

b) he can increase the rate at which it emits heat to cool it down quickly?

....

Energy

Transferring and Transforming Energy

1 When a device transfers energy, only some of the energy is usefully transferred.

a) What do we mean by **usefully transferred**?

....

b) Fill in the missing words to complete the following sentences.

The remaining energy is .... in a non-useful way. It is referred to as

.... energy.

2 Which one of the following statements is **not** true? Tick the correct option.

A The energy transformed by a drill becomes increasingly spread out (dissipated) ☐

B The energy transformed by a drill becomes difficult to use for further energy transformations ☐

C The energy transformed by a drill makes the surroundings a little warmer ☐

D The energy transformed by a drill is destroyed ☐

Efficiency

3 A standard light bulb is not very efficient. Most of the electrical energy is transformed into what type of energy? ....

4 a) If a device has an input of 100J/s, and 25J/s is transformed usefully to another form of energy, what is the device's efficiency? Tick the correct option.

A 25% ☐ **B** 50% ☐

C 75% ☐ **D** 4% ☐

b) A fluorescent tube works at 50% efficiency. If it has 50J/s of electrical energy input, what will be its light output? Tick the correct option.

A 25J/s ☐ **B** 100J/s ☐

C 200J/s ☐ **D** 50J/s ☐

c) A laptop can convert 400J of electrical energy to 240J of useful light and sound. What percentage of the energy is converted non-usefully (or wasted)? Tick the correct option.

A 60% ☐ **B** 40% ☐

C 24% ☐ **D** 50% ☐

Energy Transformation and Transfer

Energy Transformation

1

1

2

3

4

These devices transfer electrical energy in different ways.
Match statements **A**, **B**, **C** and **D**, with the labels **1–4** on the devices. Enter the appropriate number in the boxes provided.

A Movement (kinetic) energy ☐ **B** Heat (thermal) energy ☐

C Light energy ☐ **D** Sound energy ☐

Energy Transfer

2 **a)** Choose the correct words from the options given to complete the following sentences.

decreased	**National Grid**	**pylon**	**wattage**
voltage	**unaltered**	**distribution grid**	**increased**

The system of pylons that carries the generated electricity from the power station to our homes is called the .... Transformers are used to change the .... of the current. If a step-up transformer is used, it is .... If a step-down transformer is used, it is ....

b) Circle the correct option in the following sentence.

Before the electrical energy reaches our homes its voltage needs to be **stepped up / stepped down**.

3 What type of electricity do we use in our homes? Tick the correct option.

A Direct current ☐ **B** Alternative current ☐

C Alternating current ☐ **D** AC/DC ☐

Energy Transformation and Transfer

Reducing Energy Loss

1 How can energy loss in power lines be reduced? Tick the correct option.

A Increasing the current, decreasing the voltage ▢
B Increasing the voltage, decreasing the current ▢
C Increasing current and increasing the voltage ▢
D Decreasing current and decreasing the voltage ▢

2 Fill in the missing words to complete the sentence below.

For domestic use, electricity needs to be transmitted at a .... voltage and a .... current.

Energy Calculations

3 **a)** What is the unit used to measure energy transfer from the mains? Tick the correct option.

A kilowatt-hour, kWh ▢
B kilowatt, kW ▢
C joules per hour, J/h ▢
D watts, W ▢

b) What is the standard calculation used to find the total cost of energy transferred from the mains?

....

c) A 3kW electric fire is switched on for 2 hours. How much does it cost to use if a unit of electricity costs 5p? Tick the correct option.

A 3p ▢
B 30p ▢
C 300p ▢
D 1.2p ▢

d) A 7kW electric shower is used for 30 minutes. What is the cost of using this if a unit of electrical energy costs 6p? Tick the correct option.

A 21p ▢
B 35p ▢
C 42p ▢
D 1260p ▢

e) A 2kW hairdryer is used for 15 minutes every day. What is the total cost of using the hairdryer for a week if a unit of electricity costs 7p?

....

....

Fuels

1. Fill in the missing word to complete the following sentence.

   Fuels are substances which release useful amounts of energy when they are ....

Non-Renewable Energy Sources

2. What is the definition of a non-renewable energy source?

   ....

3. Is the following statement **true** or **false**?

   Wood is a fossil fuel and is non-renewable. ....

4. **a)** Fill in the missing words to complete the following passage.

   Nuclear fuel is used to generate electricity. A .... is used to generate heat by nuclear .... A heat exchanger transfers .... energy from the .... to the .... The water turns to .... and drives the ....

   b) Which of the following are nuclear fuels? Tick the **two** correct options.

   A Coal ☐ **B** Uranium ☐
   C Oil ☐ **D** Hydrogen ☐
   E Propane ☐ **F** Plutonium ☐

   c) Circle the correct options in the following sentences.

   Nuclear fuels produce energy through a process called **fusion / fission**. Nuclear particles are released, which **fuse / collide** with the nuclei of other atoms, causing them to **grow / split**. This causes a **chain / finite** reaction that generates huge amounts of energy.

5. Which of the following could not be used as fuel for a power station? Tick the correct option.

   A Oil ☐ **B** Gas ☐
   C Uranium ☐ **D** Water ☐

Energy Sources

Non-Renewable Energy Sources

1 **a)** Below is a list of statements about coal as an energy source. Tick the statements that are disadvantages.

A Cheap and easy to obtain ☐

B Burning produces carbon dioxide ☐

C Coal-fired power stations are quick to start up ☐

D Sulfur in coal contributes to acid rain ☐

b) Give one other disadvantage of using coal as a fuel.

....

2 **a)** Below is a list of statements about gas as an energy source. Tick the statements that are advantages.

A Burning produces carbon dioxide ☐

B Expensive pipelines are needed to transport it ☐

C Sources are easy to locate ☐

D Gas-fired power stations are the quickest to start up ☐

b) Give one other advantage of using gas as a fuel.

....

3 Which of the following is a valid argument against nuclear power stations? Tick the correct option.

A They have high fuel costs ☐

B They produce gases that pollute the atmosphere ☐

C They have high decommissioning costs ☐

D They need to be in constant use to work efficiently ☐

4 Which one of the following non-renewable energy sources does not produce carbon dioxide and sulfur dioxide? Tick the correct option.

A Oil ☐ **B** Gas ☐

C Nuclear ☐ **D** Coal ☐

5 Describe **two** advantages of using nuclear fuel instead of gas, coal and oil.

a) ....

b) ....

Renewable Energy Sources

1 What is the definition of a renewable energy source?

2 Many renewable energy sources are powered by the Sun or the Moon.

a) **i)** Fill in the missing word to complete the following sentence.

The gravitational pull of the Moon creates ....

ii) Name one method of generating energy that relies on this.

b) **i)** Fill in the missing word to complete the following sentence.

The Sun causes convection currents, which result in ....

ii) Name one method of generating energy that relies on this.

3 Which type of power station involves the damming of a river flowing in an upland valley? Tick the correct option.

A Nodding duck wave generator ☐ **B** Tidal barrage ☐

C Geothermal power station ☐ **D** Hydro-electric power station ☐

4 In some volcanic areas hot water and steam rise naturally to the surface of the Earth. The steam can be used to drive turbines. Which type of renewable energy source is this describing? Tick the correct option.

A Hydro-electric ☐ **B** Tidal ☐

C Wind ☐ **D** Geothermal ☐

5 **a)** Explain how nodding ducks are used to generate electrical energy.

b) Explain how a tidal barrage is used to generate electrical energy.

Energy Sources

Renewable Energy Sources

1 **a)** Draw lines between the boxes to match the energy sources with their advantages.

Source	Advantages
Wind	Fast start-up time
Hydro-electric	Can produce electricity in remote location
Tidal	Can be built offshore
Solar	Barrage water can be released when electricity demand is high

b) Draw lines between the boxes to match the energy sources with their disadvantages.

Source	Disadvantages
Wind	A hazard to shipping
Hydro-electric	Dependent on intensity of light
Tidal	Causes noise and visual pollution
Solar	Must be adequate rainfall in the region where the reservoir is

2 Which of the following statements is **not** true about a wave-driven power station? Tick the correct option.

A It can destroy habitats ☐

B No pollutant gases are produced ☐

C Variations of tides and waves affect output ☐

D A lot of fuel is used ☐

3 Which of the following statements is an advantage that wind power has over nuclear power? Tick the correct option.

A Wind power releases less CO_2 into the atmosphere ☐

B Wind power releases less SO_2 into the atmosphere ☐

C Wind turbines do not produce any dangerous waste ☐

D Wind turbines take up less space when producing the same amount of electrical energy ☐

Electromagnetic Radiation

Electromagnetic Radiation

1. Put the following four types of electromagnetic radiation in order of increasing wavelength. Write the numbers in the boxes provided (where **1** has the shortest wavelength and **4** has the longest wavelength).

   A Infra red rays ☐ **B** Gamma waves ☐

   C Radio waves ☐ **D** Ultraviolet rays ☐

2. Which of the following statements is true? Tick the correct option.

   A No electromagnetic radiation can be seen by the human eye ☐

   B All electromagnetic radiation is visible to the human eye ☐

   C All electromagnetic radiation can travel across a vacuum ☐

   D Only some of the parts of the electromagnetic spectrum can travel across a vacuum ☐

3. Choose the correct words from the options given to complete the following sentences.

   frequency **vacuum** **medium** **intensity** **energy**

   a) All electromagnetic waves can travel across a .... because they do not need a .... , unlike sound waves.

   b) All electromagnetic waves transmit ....

   c) Each type of electromagnetic radiation differs from another in wavelength and ....

4. A wave has a wavelength of 1000m and a frequency of 300 000Hz. What is its speed? Tick the correct option.

   A 300m/s ☐ **B** 30 000m/s ☐

   C 300 000m/s ☐ **D** 300 000 000m/s ☐

5. Circle the correct options in the following sentences.

   When a wave is **reflected** / **refracted** / **absorbed** by a substance it makes the substance **move** / **hotter** / **colder** / **dissolve**.

   It may create an **alternating** / **direct** / **modified** current of the same **wavelength** / **amplitude** / **frequency** as the radiation.

Electromagnetic Radiation

Electromagnetic Radiation

1 The statements describe four uses of electromagnetic radiation. Match the types of electromagnetic wave **A**, **B**, **C** and **D** below with the statements **1–4**. Enter the appropriate number in the boxes provided.

1 Transmitting radio signals
2 Treating certain cancers
3 Transmitting satellite television channels
4 Security coding valuables

A Microwaves ▢   **B** Radio waves ▢

C X-rays ▢   **D** Ultraviolet rays ▢

2 Draw lines between the boxes to match each part of the electromagnetic spectrum to its correct description.

Radio waves	Give images of broken bones, as they pass easily through soft tissue
Microwaves	Kill cancerous cells and bacteria on food, but even exposure to low doses can cause cancer
Infra red rays	Absorbed by the skin and felt as heat
Ultraviolet rays	Used by mobile phone networks
X-rays	Responsible for security coding
Gamma rays	High levels of exposure for short periods can increase body temperature, causing tissue damage

3 Which parts of the electromagnetic spectrum can be used for communications?

....

4 Microwaves are absorbed by the water particles in the food. What happens to the energy from the microwaves? Tick the correct option.

A It is emitted as light or sound energy ▢
B It increases the potential energy of the water particles ▢
C It increases the kinetic energy of the water particles ▢
D It decreases the kinetic energy of the water particles ▢

Electromagnetic Wave Communication

1 Explain briefly how electromagnetic waves carry sound as electrical signals.

....

....

....

Optical Fibres

2 **a)** Endoscopes are used by doctors to illuminate inside the ear. They make use of optical fibres. Explain why light stays inside the optical fibres.

....

b) Which of the following radiations is also used in fibre optic cables to transmit information. Tick the correct option.

A Ultraviolet ☐ **B** Microwaves ☐

C Infra red ☐ **D** Radio waves ☐

c) What are the advantages of using optical fibres over conventional copper electrical cables? Tick the **three** correct options.

A They are lighter ☐

B They are thinner and take up less space ☐

C They cannot carry as many signals as copper cable ☐

D They are affected by electrical interference ☐

E There is energy loss along copper cables ☐

Analogue and Digital Signals

3 Fill in the missing words to complete the sentences below.

A signal that continually varies its amplitude is an .... signal. These signals are more prone to interference than digital signals because they can't ignore .... Digital signals can be .... by computers unlike analogue signals. Digital signals only use on and ....

☐

Radiation

Isotopes

1 **a)** Fill in the labels A and B on the drawing of an atom.

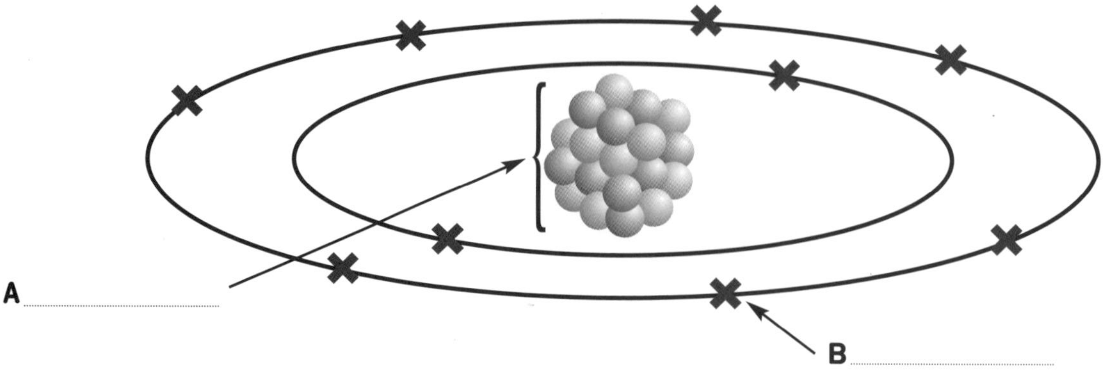

b) What is the nucleus of an atom made up of?

Radiation

2 Circle the correct options in the following sentences.

a) A form of an element with the same number of protons but a different number of neutrons is called an **ion / isotope**.

b) When a radioactive particle collides with an atom, it can remove electrons and therefore create **ions / isotopes**.

c) A radioactive particle containing 2 protons and 2 neutrons is a(n) **alpha / beta** particle.

3 **a)** What type of radiation consists of high-energy electrons emitted from the nucleus?

b) What type of radiation is not a particle but an electromagnetic wave?

4 Match statements **A**, **B**, **C** and **D** with the absorbers **1–4** below. Enter the appropriate number in the boxes provided.

1 Lead **2** Thick concrete **3** Paper **4** A few cm of aluminium

A Needed to absorb gamma radiation ☐

B All that is needed to absorb alpha radiation ☐

C Needs to be several centimetres thick to absorb gamma radiation ☐

D All that is needed to absorb beta radiation ☐

Electric and Magnetic Fields

1 a) Which types of radiation are deflected by electric fields and magnetic fields?

b) Why is this?

2 Which of the following statements about gamma radiation are true? Tick the correct options.

- **A** It is not deflected by electric fields
- **B** It is deflected by magnetic fields
- **C** It is an electromagnetic wave
- **D** It travels faster than visible light in a vacuum

Common Uses of Radiation

3 It is sometimes necessary to inject hospital patients with radioactive tracers. What is the purpose of injecting the tracer into the patient? Tick the correct option.

- **A** To track the patient's movements around the hospital
- **B** To make the patient sleepy in preparation for an operation
- **C** To track the movement of substances around the patient's body
- **D** To find out the patient's blood group

4 Give two common uses of gamma radiation.

a)

b)

5 Briefly describe how beta radiation is used in paper making.

Revision Guide Reference: Page 28

Radiation

Acute Radiation Dangers

1 Fill in the missing words to complete the sentences below.

a) Radiation damage to cells in organs can cause .... The larger the dose of radiation, the .... the risk.

b) The damaging effect of radiation depends on whether the source is .... or .... the body.

2 **a)** Which type of radiation is not a problem to humans if the source is outside the body? Tick the correct option.

A Alpha ☐ **B** Beta ☐

C Gamma ☐ **D** Alpha and beta ☐

b) Explain your answer to part a).

....

c) Which type of radiation is most dangerous to humans when they are exposed to emissions from an external source?

....

3 Although exposure to radiation carries a risk of cancer, alpha radiation is often used to treat mouth cancer. Explain why.

....

....

4 Which of the following are good precautions to take to protect a worker in a power station or factory from external exposure to radioactivity? Tick the **three** correct options.

A Label all equipment with radioactivity stickers ☐

B Avoid direct handling of the radioactive sources ☐

C Site all power stations and factories using radioactive sources well away from towns ☐

D Minimise exposure time and distance from the source of the radiation ☐

E Use protective shields, screens and containers ☐

F Do not carry instruments (e.g. a Geiger-Muller counter) to measure radiation levels ☐

Half-Life

1 Material from something that has once been alive can be dated by measuring its radioactivity. This is because all living things contain some radioactive carbon-14 atoms. Once a living thing dies it cannot absorb any more carbon-14. Carbon-14 decays by emitting beta particles and it has a half-life of 5730 years. This process is called carbon dating.

a) i) Which of the following could be dated by using carbon-14 measurements? Tick the correct option.

A An iron horseshoe ☐

B A leather belt ☐

C A gold and silver piece of jewellery ☐

D A Roman coin ☐

ii) Explain your answer to part i).

....

....

b) A piece of charcoal from a Stone Age campfire contains 16 billion carbon-14 atoms. Approximately how many carbon-14 atoms would it have contained just under 6000 years ago?

....

c) What is a beta particle emitted from an atom of carbon-14? Tick the correct option.

A A decayed neutron ☐

B A helium nucleus ☐

C An electron from the inner part (the nucleus) of an atom ☐

D An orbiting electron from the outer part of an atom ☐

2 Why should a radioactive isotope have a short half-life if it is used as a tracer in someone's bloodstream?

....

....

3 What does the term **half-life** mean?

....

☐

The Universe

Observing the Universe

1 Match statements **A**, **B**, **C** and **D** with the advantages and disadvantages **1–4** below. Enter the appropriate number in the boxes provided.

1 Can be used 24 hours a day

2 Cheaper to build, service and repair

3 Can only be used at night and if the skies are clear

4 Expensive to build, maintain and repair

A An advantage of an optical telescope in space

B An advantage of an optical telescope on Earth

C A disadvantage of an optical telescope in space

D A disadvantage of an optical telescope on Earth

Telescopes

2 Draw lines between the boxes to match each description with the correct type of telescope.

Contains a parabolic glass mirror	Radio
Orbits the Earth	Reflecting
Contains two convex (converging) lenses	Refracting
Has a large (non-glass) parabolic dish and a receiver	Space

3 Radio telescopes need to be very large compared to optical telescopes. Why is this?

Using Telescopes

4 Why are many telescopes placed on the top of mountains and in areas with low levels of pollution?

Red Shift

1 **a)** Which of the following emit light, which provides possible evidence about the origin of the Universe? Tick the correct option.

A Planets ☐ **B** Moons ☐

C Comets ☐ **D** Galaxies ☐

b) The light emitted in part a) displays 'red shift'. What does this mean?

....

....

c) What do scientists suggest that red shift provides evidence of? Tick the correct option.

A The theory of evolution ☐

B Life elsewhere in the Universe ☐

C Global warming ☐

D The Big Bang theory ☐

2 Fill in the missing words to complete the sentences below.

Light that reaches the Earth from distant stars and galaxies is shifted .... the red end of the electromagnetic spectrum. This is evidence that the galaxies are moving .... from the Earth. This suggests that the Universe is ....

3 The red shift effect is more exaggerated in the galaxies that are furthest away. What does this suggest?

....

4 Which answer correctly describes the movement of the galaxies at the present time, **a)** relative to the Earth, **b)** relative to each other. Tick the correct option.

A **a)** moving away, **b)** moving closer ☐

B **a)** moving away, **b)** moving away ☐

C **a)** moving closer, **b)** moving closer ☐

D **a)** moving closer, **b)** moving away ☐

Speed

Speed

1 What two measurements must you take to calculate the speed of an object? Tick the correct option.

A Distance and direction of travel ▢
B Time and direction of travel ▢
C Distance and time ▢
D Acceleration and direction of travel ▢

2 You can calculate speed using the formula:

$$\textbf{Speed (m/s)} = \frac{\textbf{Distance travelled (m)}}{\textbf{Time taken (s)}}$$

Jill ran 1500m in 5 minutes and 20 seconds. What was Jill's average speed?

....

Distance–Time Graphs

3 a) The graph shows the journey of a runner. Fill in the missing values to complete the following sentences.

In 30 minutes he runs .... km.

After travelling .... km he rests for .... minutes.

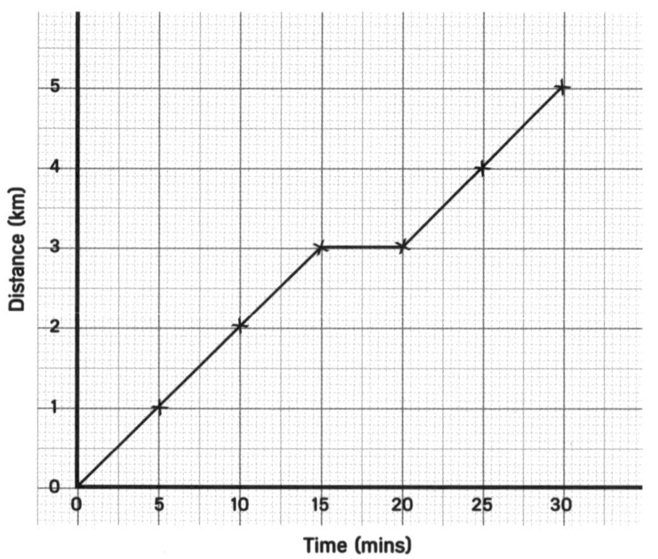

b) What was the runner's speed in km/h for the first 15 minutes? Tick the correct option.

A 12km/h ▢
B 0.2km/h ▢
C 10km/h ▢
D 3km/h ▢

Velocity

4 Explain the difference between velocity and speed.

....

....

Acceleration

Acceleration

1 Circle the correct options in the following sentences.

a) Acceleration is the rate of change of an object's **distance / time / velocity / direction**.

b) To work out the acceleration of a moving object, you need to know the change in **distance / time / velocity / direction** and the **time taken / direction / distance travelled** for this change to occur.

2 What is the formula used to calculate acceleration? You should specify the unit of measure for each variable.

....

....

Velocity–Time Graphs

3 a) Look at the four graphs. Which graph shows an object accelerating at $3 m/s^2$? Tick the correct option.

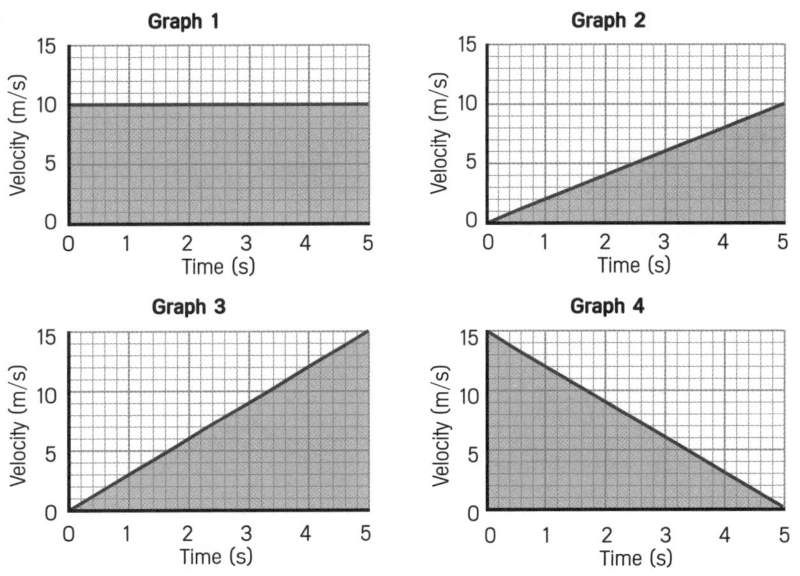

A Graph 1 ☐

B Graph 2 ☐

C Graph 3 ☐

D Graph 4 ☐

b) What does the area under a velocity–time graph show? Tick the correct option.

A The average velocity of the object during its journey ☐

B The total distance travelled by the object during its journey ☐

C The average acceleration of the object during its journey ☐

D The total time for the journey ☐

c) Circle the correct option in the following sentence.

The total distance travelled by the object in Graph 1 is **5m / 10m / 15m / 50m**.

Forces

Forces

1 Fill in the missing words to complete the following sentences.

Forces are pushes or .... They are measured in .... and may vary in size and act in different ....

Friction

2 James is riding his jet ski at a constant speed of 15m/s. The jet ski's engines provide a forward force. Is there a force acting in the opposite direction? Tick the correct option.

- **A** Yes, the jet ski's weight opposes the force from the engines ☐
- **B** Yes, upthrust opposes the force from the jet ski's engines ☐
- **C** Yes, friction opposes the force from the jet ski's engines ☐
- **D** No, the jet ski is travelling forwards so the forward force must be unbalanced ☐

Stopping Distance

3 The stopping distance is the sum of the thinking distance and the braking distance. Which of the following factors would increase the **thinking** distance? Tick the **two** correct options.

- **A** A vehicle that is well-maintained ☐
- **B** A vehicle that is travelling fast ☐
- **C** Good visibility ☐
- **D** An icy road ☐
- **E** A driver who is tired ☐
- **F** A driver who is under the influence of alcohol ☐

How Forces Affect Movement

4 A hawk is flying with a constant velocity. However, if an unbalanced force acts on the hawk, its velocity will change. What noticeable effect might this have? Tick the **three** correct options.

- **A** The hawk might speed up ☐
- **B** The hawk might slow down ☐
- **C** The hawk might continue flying at a constant speed, in a straight line ☐
- **D** The hawk might continue flying at a constant speed, but change direction ☐
- **E** The hawk's weight might increase ☐
- **F** The hawk's weight might decrease ☐

Force, Mass and Acceleration

1 A hockey player hits a puck with a small force, making it accelerate. Circle the correct options in the following sentences.

a) A puck that's hit with a bigger force will experience **a smaller / the same / a greater** acceleration.

b) A puck with a greater mass that's hit with the same force will experience **a smaller / the same / a greater** acceleration.

2 What is the formula that describes the relationship between force, mass and acceleration? You should state the unit of measure for each variable.

3 What is a newton (N)?

4 A car is moving at a constant speed of 30m/s. The total mass of the car and the driver is 1000kg.

a) If the driving force is 3000N, what is the value of the frictional force?

b) If the driver increases the driving force to 4000N, what is the acceleration of the car?

5 A motorcycle is moving along a straight road. The total mass of the motorcyclist and the bike is 250kg. The motorcycle accelerates at $2m/s^2$. Calculate the force needed to produce this acceleration.

6 Will the car or the lorry have the greatest acceleration? Explain your answer.

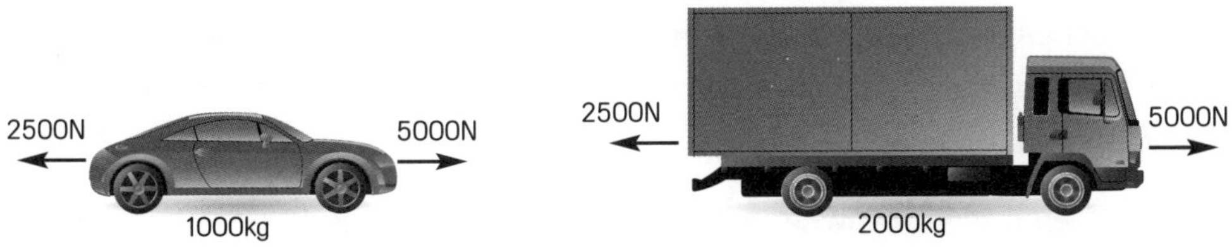

Terminal Velocity

1 What is meant by the term 'terminal velocity'?

....

....

2 **a)** The graph shows the velocity of a skydiver against time.

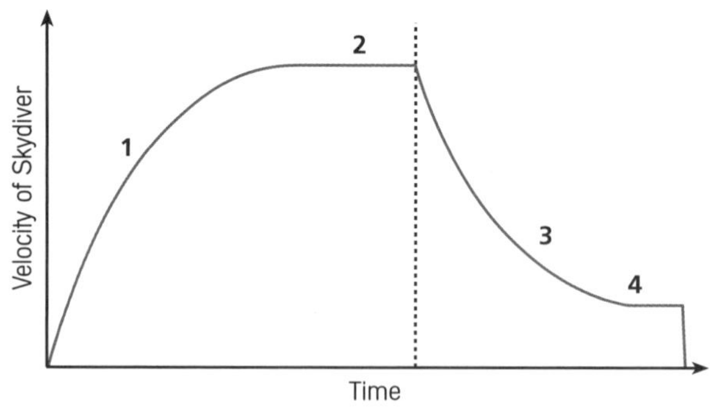

Match statements **A**, **B**, **C** and **D** with the labels **1**–**4** on the graph. Write the appropriate numbers in the boxes provided.

A The skydiver's speed is decreasing ☐

B The skydiver's parachute is open and his speed is constant ☐

C The skydiver's speed is constant. He has not yet opened his parachute ☐

D The skydiver's speed is increasing ☐

b) Circle the correct options in the following sentences.

i) A skydiver jumps from a helicopter, which is hovering high above the ground. At the instant he jumps **his mass / his weight / air resistance** is equal to zero, so **his mass / his weight / air resistance** causes him to accelerate downwards.

ii) As he accelerates downwards, the upward force of **his mass / his weight / air resistance** gradually increases.

iii) The skydiver reaches a constant speed when the upward force is **smaller than / equal to / greater than** the downward force. At this point the skydiver has reached his **ultimate velocity / top velocity / terminal velocity**.

3 After a few minutes of freefall, the downward force acting on a skydiver is 600N. The upward force of air resistance is also 600N. What is the resultant force acting on the skydiver?

....

Work and Kinetic Energy

Work

1 When Matilda rolls a ball to Pablo, work is done on the ball. What does this mean? Tick the correct option.

- **A** The ball heats up slightly (due to friction) as it rolls ☐
- **B** Matilda accelerates the ball ☐
- **C** Matilda exerts a force on the ball ☐
- **D** Matilda transfers energy to the ball ☐

2 An elephant is being transported between zoos. A crane is used to lift with a force equal to the elephant's weight: 20kN. It lifts the elephant a vertical distance of 6 metres. Complete the following sentence.

The crane has done .... kJ of work on the elephant.

3 Which of the devices below can store elastic potential energy? Tick the **three** correct options.

- **A** A wind-up toy train ☐
- **B** A petrol tank ☐
- **C** A sling-shot ☐
- **D** A bungee cord ☐
- **E** A battery ☐
- **F** A grandfather clock, powered by falling weights ☐

Kinetic Energy

4 **a)** What is kinetic energy?

....

b) A greyhound runs at a constant speed of 20m/s. What happens to its kinetic energy? Tick the correct option.

- **A** It has no kinetic energy ☐
- **B** Its kinetic energy decreases, due to friction ☐
- **C** As it runs for longer, its kinetic energy increases ☐
- **D** Its speed isn't changing, so its kinetic energy doesn't change ☐

HT

5 Racing horses, greyhounds and hares can all reach speeds of around 20m/s. Of the three, the horse has the biggest mass and the hare has the smallest mass. If all three animals are running at 20m/s, which will have the least kinetic energy?

.... ☐

Momentum

Momentum

1 **a)** What is momentum?

b) What two things does momentum depend on?

i)

ii)

2 Write down the equation for calculating momentum.

3 A jogger has a mass of 80kg and is running at a velocity of 0.4m/s. What is the jogger's momentum? Tick the correct option. (You can use the line below for your calculations.)

A 320kg m/s

B 200kg m/s

C 20kg m/s

D 32kg m/s

4 A truck is moving with a velocity of 18m/s. Calculate its mass if it has a momentum of 61 000kg m/s.

Magnitude and Direction

5 A tennis ball has a mass of 0.06kg. When it's served, it moves away from the racket with a velocity of 30m/s. Circle the correct options in the following sentences.

a) The momentum of the ball after the serve is **0.6 / 1.2 / 1.8 / 3.0** kg m/s.

b) The ball is returned by the other player at a velocity of -25m/s. On its return, the momentum of the ball is **-0.6 / -0.9 / -1.2 / -1.5** kg m/s.

6 A car of mass 1200kg is travelling at a velocity of 15m/s. What happens to its velocity and its momentum if the car then travels in the opposite direction with a speed of 15m/s?

Letts and Lonsdale

GCSE Success

Workbook Answer Booklet

AQA Physics

Answer Booklet

GCSE Physics AQA

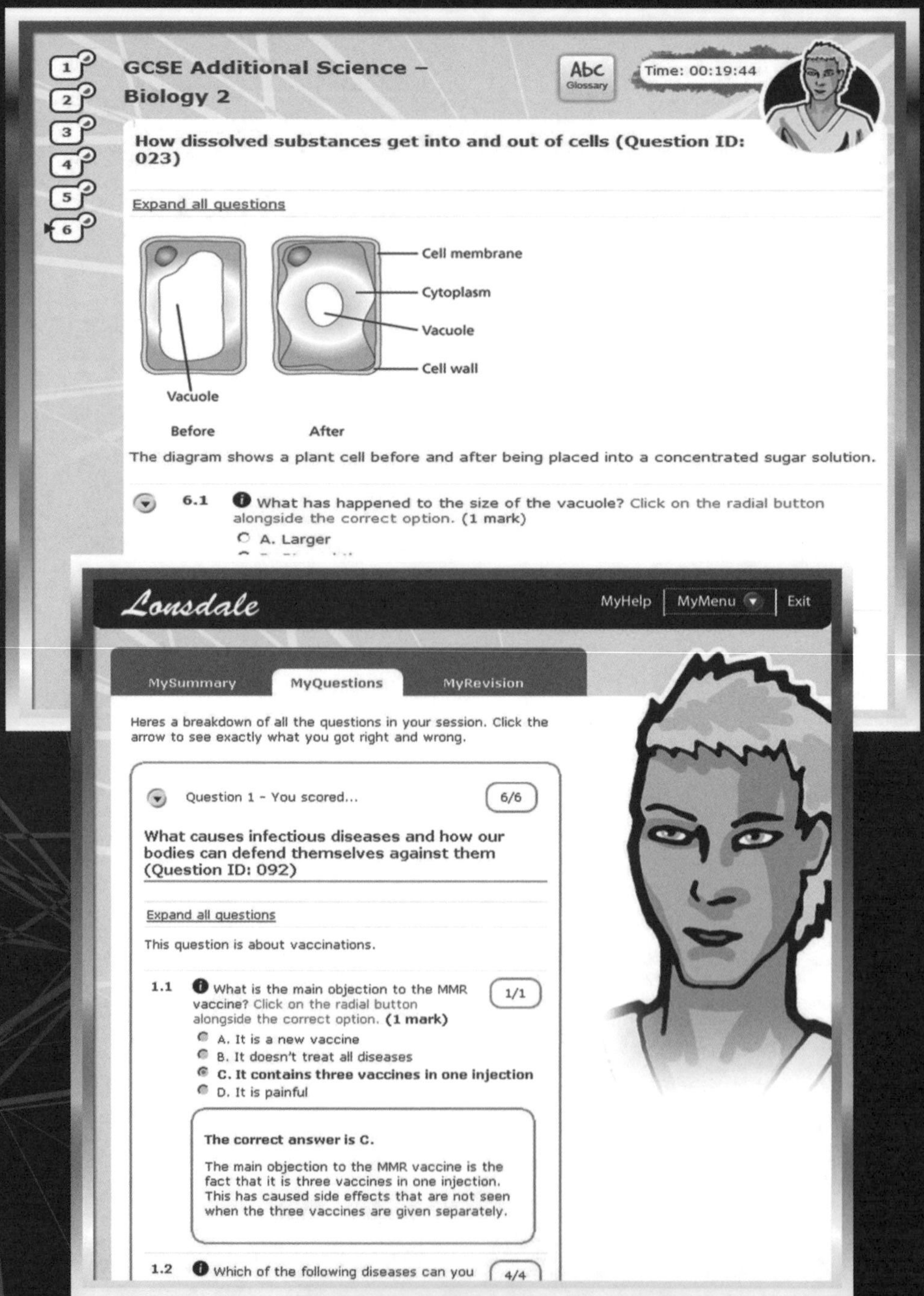

GCSE Additional Science – Biology 2
Abc Glossary
Time: 00:19:44
How dissolved substances get into and out of cells (Question ID: 023)
Expand all questions
Cell membrane
Cytoplasm
Vacuole
Cell wall
Vacuole
Before
After
The diagram shows a plant cell before and after being placed into a concentrated sugar solution.
6.1 What has happened to the size of the vacuole? Click on the radial button alongside the correct option. (1 mark)
A. Larger
Lonsdale
MyHelp
MyMenu
Exit
MySummary
MyQuestions
MyRevision
Heres a breakdown of all the questions in your session. Click the arrow to see exactly what you got right and wrong.
Question 1 - You scored...
6/6
What causes infectious diseases and how our bodies can defend themselves against them (Question ID: 092)
Expand all questions
This question is about vaccinations.
1.1 What is the main objection to the MMR vaccine? Click on the radial button alongside the correct option. (1 mark)
1/1
A. It is a new vaccine
B. It doesn't treat all diseases
C. It contains three vaccines in one injection
D. It is painful
The correct answer is C.
The main objection to the MMR vaccine is the fact that it is three vaccines in one injection. This has caused side effects that are not seen when the three vaccines are given separately.
1.2 Which of the following diseases can you
4/4

AQA Physics Success Workbook Answers

Page 4

1. a) convection
b) conduction

2. a) conduction
b) convection
c) convection

3. B

4. a) A
b) B

5. convection

Page 5

1. electromagnetic waves

2. No particles of matter are involved

3. a) A and F
b) A, C and D

4. faster

5. a) Put a shiny material (e.g. foil) around it
b) Put a black material around it

Page 6

1. a) To where it's wanted and in the form that's wanted.
b) transformed; wasted

2. D

3. Heat

4. a) A
b) A
c) B

Page 7

1. A 3, B 1, C 2, D 4

2. a) National Grid; voltage; increased; decreased
b) stepped down

3. C

Page 8

1. B

2. low; high

3. a) A
b) Energy transfer = Power x Time
c) B
d) A
e) 24.5p

Page 9

1. burned

2. An energy source that can't be replaced within a lifetime.

3. False

4. a) reactor; fission; thermal; reactor; water; steam; turbines
b) B and F
c) fission; collide; split; chain

5. D

Page 10

1. a) B and D.
b) Produces more CO_2 per unit energy than oil or coal does.

2. a) C and D
b) **Any one from:** there is enough gas left for the short to medium term; doesn't produce SO_2

3. C

4. C

5. a)–b) Any two from: cost and rate of fuel is low; can be situated in sparsely populated areas; flexible in meeting demand; does not produce CO_2 or SO_2.

Page 11

1. One that will not run out.

2. a) i) tides **ii)** tidal barrage / nodding duck
b) i) wind **ii)** wind turbines

3. D

4. D

5. a) The motion of the waves rocks the 'nodding duck'. The movement is translated into a rotary motion which drives a generator.
b) As the tide comes in, the water flows through the barrage and becomes trapped. At low tide the water is released, which drives a generator.

Page 12

1. a)

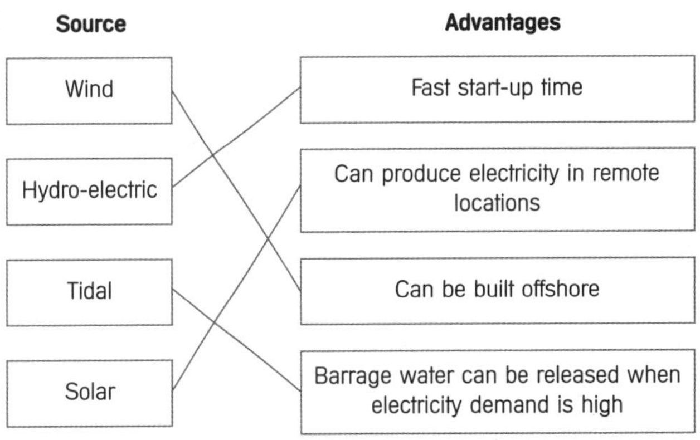

b)

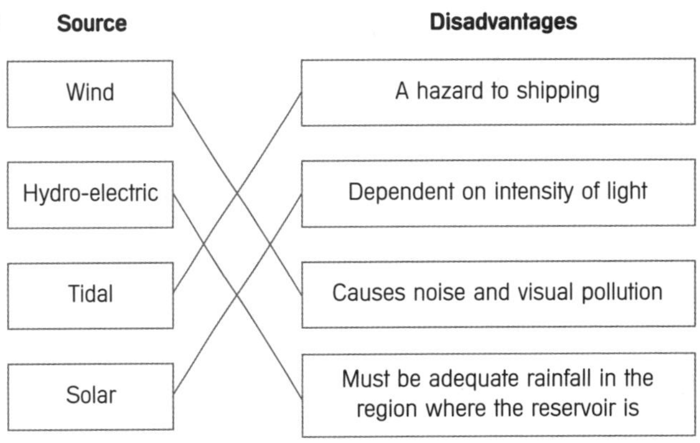

2. D

3. C

Page 13

1. A 3, B 1, C 4, D 2

2. C

3. a) vacuum; medium
b) energy
c) frequency

4. D

5. absorbed; hotter; alternating; frequency

Page 14

1. A 1, B 3, C 2, D 4

2.

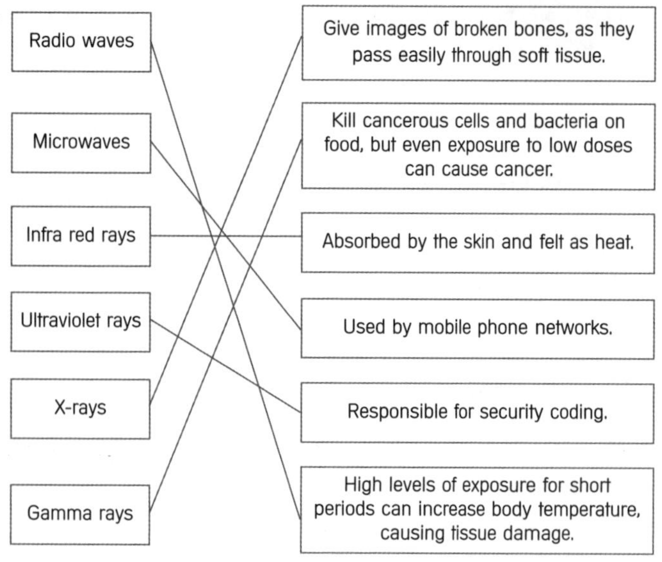

3. radio waves, microwaves, visible light, infra red rays.

4. C

Page 15

1. A 'carrier' wave carries the electrical signal from a transmitter. This produces a modulated wave. The modulated wave is picked up by the aerial in a radio. The carrier wave is then removed to leave the original signal (i.e. it is demodulated).

2. **a)** Because it is reflected off the walls of the optical fibre.
   b) C
   c) A, B and E

3. Analogue; noise; processed; off

Page 16

1. **a)** A = Nucleus, B = Electron
   b) Protons and neutrons

2. **a)** isotope
   b) ions
   c) alpha

3. **a)** beta
   b) gamma

4. A 2, B 3, C 1, D 4

Page 17

1. **a)** Alpha and beta radiation
   b) Because they are charged particles (gamma is a wave)

2. A and C

3. C

4. **a)–b) In any order:** sterilisation; treating cancer

5. A beta emitter is placed on one side of the paper, and a detector is on the other. If the paper gets too thick, less beta radiation is detected, so a signal is sent to the rollers to move closer together to reduce the thickness of the paper.

Page 18

1. **a)** cancer; greater
   b) inside; outside

2. **a)** A
   b) It cannot penetrate the body; it is stopped by the skin.
   c) Gamma

3. Alpha radiation is highly ionising to internal tissue. This means it can damage molecules inside living cells, causing the cells to die. This can be beneficial if the cells are cancerous.

4. B, D and E

Page 19

1. **a)** **i)** B **ii)** Leather is made from dead skin so it was once living.
   b) 32 billion
   c) D

2. So that the radioactivity of the tracer returns to safe levels as soon as possible, preventing it from damaging cells.

3. It is the time taken for the number of nuclei in a sample of an isotope to halve.

Page 20

1. A 1, B 2, C 4, D 3

2.

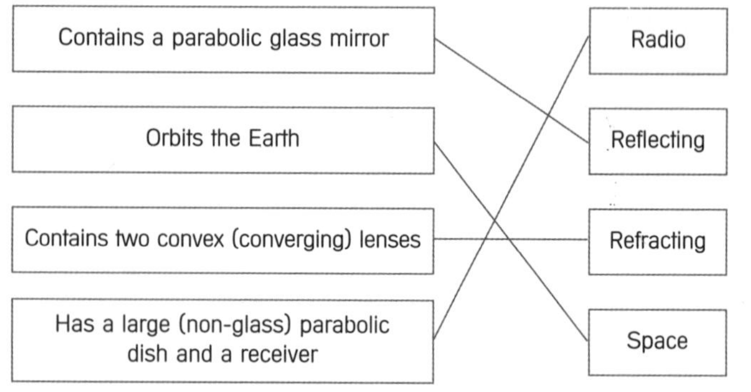

3. So they can detect very weak signals. (Radio waves have a much longer wavelength than light waves.)

4. So they are not affected by light pollution from built-up areas.

Page 21

1. **a)** D
   b) The light received from them is shifted towards the red end of the spectrum, which means they are moving away from us.
   c) D

2. towards; away; expanding

3. The further away a galaxy is, the faster it's moving away from us.

4. B

Page 22

1. C

2. 4.7m/s

3. **a)** 5; 3; 5.
   b) A

4. The velocity of an object describes its speed *in a given direction.*

Page 23

1. **a)** velocity
   b) velocity; time taken.

2. $\text{Acceleration (m/s}^2) = \dfrac{\text{Change in velocity (m/s)}}{\text{Time taken for change (s)}}$

3. **a)** C
   b) B
   c) 50m

Page 24

1. pulls; newtons (N); directions.

2. C

3. E and F

4. A, B and D

Page 25

1. **a)** a greater
   b) a smaller

2. Resultant force (N) = Mass (kg) x Acceleration (m/s^2)

3. The force needed to give a mass of one kilogram (1 kg) an acceleration of one metre per second squared ($1 m/s^2$).

4. a) 3000N
   b) Acceleration = $\frac{4000}{1000}$ = $4 m/s^2$

5. Force = 250 x 2 = 500N

6. The car, because for the same balanced force the mass is half as much.

Page 26

1. When the velocity of a falling object is no longer accelerating (i.e. it is constant) because the gravitational force is equal to the frictional forces.

2. a) A 3; B 4; C 2; D 1
   b) i) air resistance; his weight
      ii) air resistance
      iii) equal to; terminal velocity

3. Zero

Page 27

1. D

2. 120

3. A, C and D

4. a) The energy an object has because of its movement.
   b) D

5. The hare

Page 28

1. a) A measure of the state of motion of an object.
   b) i) and ii) **In any order:** The mass of the object (kg); The velocity of the object (m/s).

2. Momentum (kg m/s) = Mass (kg) x Velocity (m/s)

3. D

4. $\frac{61\ 000}{18}$ = 3389kg

5. a) 1.8
   b) -1.5

6. The velocity and momentum will both become negative.

Page 29

1. B

2. 1400kg m/s; -1400kg m/s; -1000N.

3. Reducing the force on a driver will reduce the likelihood of injury. Airbags increase the time over which the change in momentum occurs, thereby reducing the force on the driver.

4. a) 3; 6
   b) 6; 12

Page 30

1. a) D

   b) i) 24 000; 9000; 33 000
      ii) 33 000; 15

2. C

3. 0.16

Page 31

1. B

2. a) repel
   b) attract

3. a) and b) **Any two suitable answers**, e.g.: Smoke precipitator; Photocopier.

4. A 1; B 2; C 4; D 3.

Page 32

1. A 4; B 6; C 1; D 5; E 2; F 3

2. Positive

3. Any charged unearthed object can have the charge on it removed by connecting it to earth with a conductor.

4. B, C and F

5. become ionised; spark; discharge.

Page 33

1. A and C

2. a) C
   b) A

3. B and D

4. potential difference

Page 34

1. A measure of how hard it is to get a current through a component at a particular potential difference.

2. Potential difference (V) = Current (A) x Resistance (Ω)

3. 2 ohms

4. A 3; B 1; C 2

5. A 2; B 4; C 1; D 3

Page 35

1. a) parallel
   b) series

2. D

3. B

4. a) 2A
   b) 4.5V
   c) 4.5V

5. 6V

Page 36

1. 230V

2. a) alternating; direct.
   b) The number of complete cycles of reversal per second.

3. A 2; B 1; C 4; D 3.

4. Brass, because it's a good conductor.

Page 37

1. To protect appliances from overheating, causing damage, and to protect the user.

2. A

3. When the current passing through the fuse exceeds the current rating of the fuse, the fuse wire gets hot and melts, breaking the circuit.

4. A 3; B 2; C 5; D 1; E 4

5. B and D

Page 38

1. B and D

2. 72W

3. a) coulomb
   b) 30 coulombs

4. a) 900C
   b) 18W
   c) 5400J

5. greater

Page 39

1. C
2. Because an atom has the same number of protons (+1) and electrons (-1), so the overall charge is neutral (zero).
3. Atoms of the same element with different numbers of neutrons.
4. A, B and F
5. **a)** helium nucleus
   b) D

Page 40

1. C, D and E
2. **a)** Radioactive; neutral
   b) charged; ions.
3. **a) and b) In any order:** Alpha; Beta.
4. **a)–d) Any four suitable answers**, e.g.: Rocks; Volcanoes; Medical applications; Cosmic rays.
5. Because it only occurs in small doses.

Page 41

1. B
2. **a) and b) Any two suitable answers**, e.g.: The release of energy in stars; An atomic bomb exploding.
3. **a) and b) In any order:** Uranium-235; Plutonium-239.
4. A 4; B 2; C 1; D 3
5. A and D

Page 42

1. pivot
2. The turning effect of a force.
3. C
4. Moment (Nm) = Force (N) x Perpendicular distance between line of action and pivot (m)
5. increasing; increasing
6. A
7. point; suspension

Page 43

1. When an object is balanced there is a balance between the total moments of the forces turning the object in both a clockwise and anticlockwise direction.
2. 7.2N
3. B and D
4. not; moment
5. D

Page 44

1. **a) and b) Accept any two suitable answers**, e.g. A rubber ball spun on a piece of string; Spinning rides at fairgrounds; A car turning; The Earth and other planets in orbit around the Sun.
2. D
3. **a)** C
   b) A
4. **a) and b) Any two from:** Increasing the mass of the object; Increasing the speed of the object; Decreasing the radius of the circle.
5. **a)** B
   b) D

Page 45

1. **a)** reduces
   b) more
2. **a)** C
   b) **i)** True
   ii) False
   iii) False
3. **a)** C
   b) The orbit time is shorter than that of a geostationary satellite because the smaller the distance between the satellite and the planet, the shorter the orbit time.

Page 46

1. **a)** B
   b) **i)** reflected
   ii) incidence
2. **a)** D
   b) C

Page 47

1. **a)** Inverted
   b) Virtual
2. **a)** A mirror that curves inwards.
   b) A mirror that curves outwards.
3. Focus point
4. **a)** smaller; virtual; upright
   b) converge
5. **a)** A
   b) D

Page 48

1. **a)** refracts
   b) concave; convex
2. A
3. Parallel Rays of Light

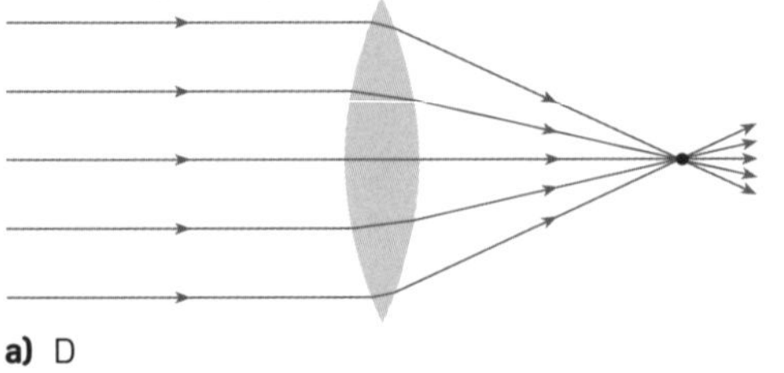

4. **a)** D
   b) smaller / nearer; nearer / smaller

Page 49

1. C
2. Waveform.
3. A
4. **a)** C
   b) pitch; pitch; higher
5. A
6. It becomes louder.

Page 50

1. C
2. C
3. reflected; boundary
4. B and C
5. D

6. **a)** Vibrations used within a liquid dislodge the dirt particles.
b) **i) and ii) In any order:** No danger of breakage; No need to take the object apart.

Page 51

1. movement

2. B

3. **a) and b) In any order:** Increasing the size of the current; Increasing the strength of the magnetic field.

4. **a) and b) In any order:** Reversing the direction of flow of the current; Reversing the direction of the magnetic field.

5. Electric motors

6. **a)** electromagnet
b) poles
c) rotates

Page 52

1. **a)** movement; current
b) Electricity

2. **a)** induced
b) complete

3. **a) and b) In any order:** Moving the magnet out of the coil; Moving the other pole of the magnet into the coil.

4. No current is induced

5. **a)** **i)** area
ii) speed
b) **i) and ii) In any order:** Increasing the strength of the magnetic field; Increasing the number of turns on the coil.

Page 53

1. A transformer changes electrical energy from one potential difference to another potential difference.

2. **a)** primary / secondary; primary / secondary; iron
b) **i)** secondary
ii) primary

3. alternating

4. **a)** greater
b) less

5. National Grid; transmission

6. Step-up transformer

Page 54

1. A

2. **a)** helium
b) energy; elements

3. 5 billion years old

4.

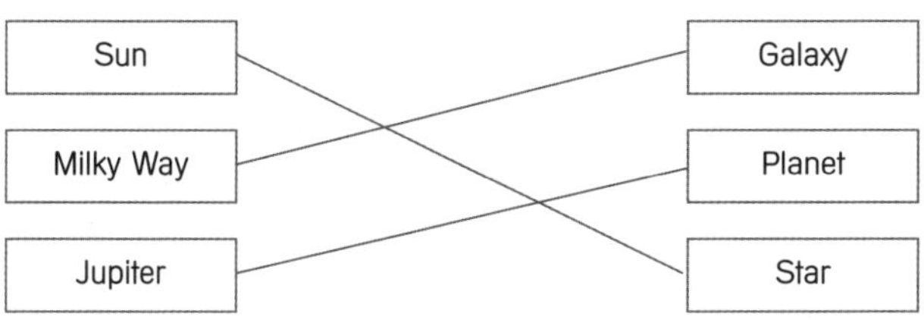

5. D

6. Radiation; gravity

Page 55

1. **a)** B
b) The red giant eventually collapses and becomes a white dwarf.

2. D

3. B

4. **a)** neutron star
b) black hole

5. **a)** Hydrogen
b) **i) and ii) In any order:** New stars; New planets

ACKNOWLEDGEMENTS

The author and publisher are grateful to the copyright holders for permission to use quoted materials and photographs.

Letts and Lonsdale
4 Grosvenor Place
London SW1X 7DL

School orders: 015395 64910
School enquiries: 015395 65921
Parent and student enquiries: 015395 64913
Email: enquiries@lettsandlonsdale.co.uk
Website: www.lettsandlonsdale.com

First published 2008

British Library Cataloguing in Publication Data. A CIP record of this book is available from the British Library.

Book concept and development: Helen Jacobs,

Editors: Katie Galloway and Ali March
Concept Design: Sarah Duxbury and Helen Jacobs
Design: Lonsdale and FiSH Books
Artwork: Lonsdale and HL Studios

Printed and bound in China

Force and Change in Momentum

1 Why does spreading out the change of momentum over a longer time reduce the risk of injury to a driver in a car crash? Tick the correct option.

A It gives the driver time to react ▢

B It reduces the maximum force on the driver ▢

C It enables the driver to steer away from the collision ▢

D It reduces the velocity of the car ▢

HT

2 Fill in the missing values to complete the following sentences.

In a crash-test laboratory, a dummy of mass 70kg hit a wall at a velocity of 20m/s. The dummy had a momentum of ______________. The dummy was brought to rest (zero velocity) in 1.4 seconds. The change of momentum of the dummy was ______________. The average force exerted on the dummy was ______________.

3 Use ideas of momentum and force to explain why airbags reduce the level of injury in a car crash.

____

____

4 **a)** Vicki kicked a stationary ball of mass 0.5kg with a force of 20N whilst her foot remained in contact with the ball for 0.15s. Fill in the missing values to complete the following sentence.

The ball left Vicki's foot with a momentum of ______________ kg m/s and a velocity of ______________ m/s.

b) Leila is a better football player than Vicki and when she kicked the same ball with the same force her foot remained in contact with the ball for 0.3s. Fill in the missing values to complete the following sentence.

The ball left Leila's foot with a momentum of ______________ kg m/s and a velocity of ______________ m/s.

Revision Guide Reference: Page 44

Collisions and Explosions

Collisions and Explosions

1 a) Collisions and explosions follow the law of conservation of momentum. What does conservation of momentum mean? Tick the correct option.

- **A** Momentum never changes
- **B** Collisions are the same as backwards explosions
- **C** The momentum of each object before a collision or explosion is the same as the momentum of each object after the collision or explosion
- **D** The total momentum of the objects involved in a collision or explosion is the same before the event as after the event

b) Look carefully at the image. In this question the momentum of each car is positive.

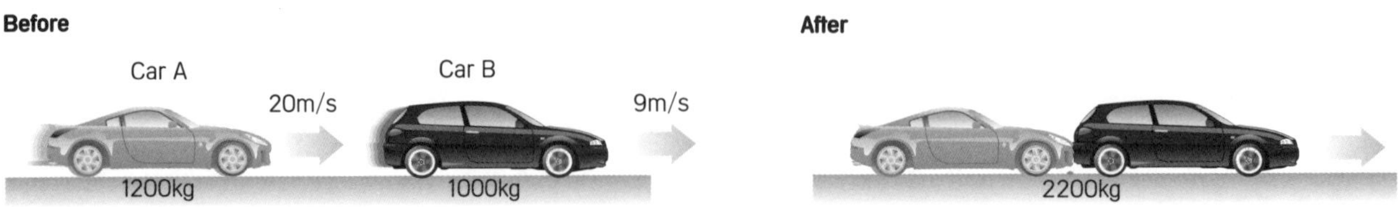

Circle the correct options in the following sentences.

i) Before the collision, Car A has a momentum of **24 000 / 9000 / 1200 / 25 000** kg m/s and Car B has a momentum of **19 000 / 2000 / 9000 / 25 000** kg m/s. The total momentum before the collision is **15 000 / 11 000 / 25 000 / 33 000** kg m/s.

ii) After the collision, the two cars move off together. Their total momentum is **15 000 / 11 000 / 25 000 / 33 000** kg m/s and they have a combined mass of 2200kg. They will move off with a velocity of **12 / 15 / 18 / 21** m/s.

2 Ali was standing on a skateboard, which wasn't moving. He caught a very heavy sports ball, which was thrown straight at him with a velocity of 18m/s. He didn't fall off the skateboard. What happened next? Tick the correct option.

- **A** Ali and the skateboard remained still
- **B** Ali, the skateboard and the ball moved with a velocity of 18m/s
- **C** Ali, the skateboard and the ball moved with a velocity of less than 18m/s
- **D** Ali, the skateboard and the ball moved with a velocity of more than 18m/s

3 Circle the correct option in the following sentence.

A cricket ball is thrown at 30m/s. Its momentum is 4.8kg m/s, so the mass of the ball is **0.12 / 0.16 / 0.20 / 0.24** kg.

Static Electricity

1 When a Perspex rod is rubbed with a cloth the rod becomes positively charged. Why is this? Tick the correct option.

A The rod has gained protons ☐

B The rod has lost electrons ☐

C The cloth has lost protons ☐

D The rod has gained protons and lost electrons ☐

Repulsion and Attraction

2 Circle the correct options in the following sentences.

a) Materials with the same charge **attract / repel** each other.

b) Materials with different charges **attract / repel** each other.

The Uses of Static

3 Give two examples of devices that use electrostatic charges.

a) ....

b) ....

Electrostatic Smoke Precipitator

4 The diagram shows a cross-section of an electrostatic smoke precipitator.

Match statements **A**, **B**, **C** and **D**, with the labels **1**–**4** on the diagram.

Write the appropriate number in the boxes provided.

A Positively charged particles collect at negative plates at the side of the chimney ☐

B Positively charged particles repel each other towards the sides of the chimney ☐

C Smoke and waste gases ☐

D Positive grid charges particles as they pass through ☐

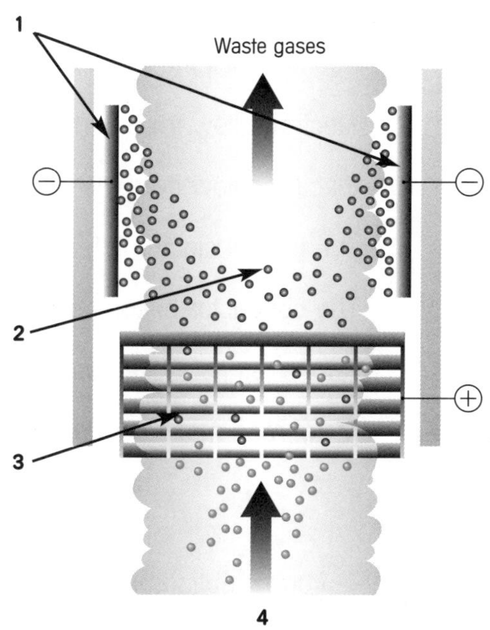

Static Electricity

The Photocopier

1. The following statements describe how a photocopier works. They are in the wrong order. Number the statements **1–6** to show the correct order.

   A Charged impression on the plate attracts tiny specs of black powder ☐

   B Paper is heated to fix the final image ☐

   C Copying plate is electrically charged ☐

   D Powder is transferred from the plate to the paper ☐

   E Image of the page to be copied is projected onto the plate ☐

   F Charge leaks away due to light, leaving an electrostatic impression of the page ☐

2. Does the electrically charged plate in a photocopier usually carry a positive or negative charge?

   ....

Discharge of Static Electricity

3. Briefly describe what is meant by 'discharging static electricity'.

   ....

   ....

4. Which of the following statements describe what happens when a conductor touches a negatively charged dome? Tick the **three** correct options.

   A Electrons flow from earth to the dome ☐

   B Electrons flow from the dome to earth ☐

   C The flow of electrons is an electric current ☐

   D The conductor becomes permanently charged ☐

   E Rubber strips make good conductors ☐

   F Metal rods make good conductors ☐

HT

5. Circle the correct options in the following sentence.

   If the potential difference between an object and a nearby, earthed conductor rises high enough, the surrounding air molecules **are destroyed / become ionised / disappear** and there's a **fusion / chemical reaction / spark** as **recharge / discharge / uncharge** occurs. ☐

Circuits

1 Which of the following statements about electric circuits are true? Tick the **two** correct options.

- **A** An ammeter measures the current of the circuit ☐
- **B** A voltmeter measures the current of the circuit ☐
- **C** An electric current flows if there's a potential difference across the ends of a component ☐
- **D** An ammeter measures the resistance of the circuit ☐

2 **a)** Circuit 1 contains 1 battery and 1 lamp. Circuit 2 contains 1 battery and 2 lamps. Compared to circuit 1, how brightly will the lamps in circuit 2 light up? Tick the correct option.

- **A** The same brightness ☐
- **B** Brighter ☐
- **C** Less bright ☐
- **D** You can't tell ☐

b) Circuit 3 contains 2 batteries and 2 lamps. Compared to circuit 1, how brightly will the lamps in circuit 3 light up? Tick the correct option.

- **A** The same brightness ☐
- **B** Brighter ☐
- **C** Less bright ☐
- **D** You can't tell ☐

3 Which of the following factors determine the amount of current that flows through a component? Tick the **two** correct options.

- **A** The thickness of the wires used in the circuit ☐
- **B** The potential difference across the component ☐
- **C** Whether a voltmeter is connected or not ☐
- **D** The resistance of the component ☐
- **E** The length of the wires used in the circuit ☐
- **F** The distance between the component and the power source ☐

4 Fill in the missing word(s) to complete the following sentence.

The greater the resistance of a component, the greater the ....

needed to maintain a particular current.

Electric Circuits

Resistance

1 Briefly explain what resistance in a circuit is.

2 What is the formula that you would use to calculate potential difference?

3 A circuit has a potential difference of 6V and a current of 3A. What is the resistance?

Resistors

4 Below are three current–voltage graphs.

1

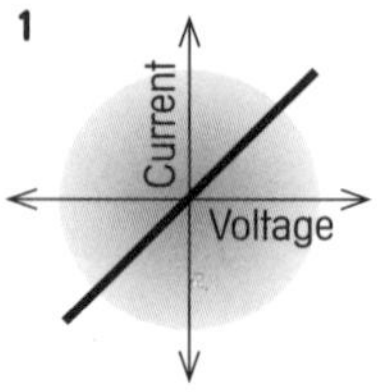

2

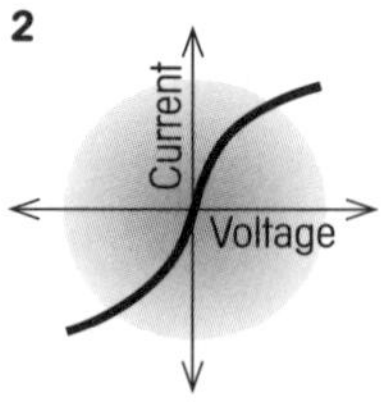

3

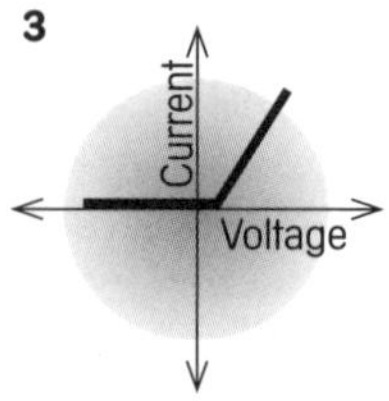

Which graph corresponds to each of the following components? Enter the appropriate numbers in the boxes provided.

A A diode

B A resistor at a constant temperature

C A filament lamp

5 Match statements **A**, **B**, **C** and **D** with the resistors **1**–**4** listed below. Write the appropriate numbers in the boxes provided.

1 Light dependent resistor

2 Thermistor

3 Diode

4 Filament lamp

A Resistance decreases as the temperature of the resistor increases

B Resistance increases as the temperature of the resistor increases

C Resistance decreases as light intensity increases

D The resistor has a very high resistance in one direction

Series and Parallel Circuits

1 Fill in the missing words to complete the following sentences.

a) A circuit in which all the components are connected separately in their own loop, going from one end of the battery to the other, is called a .... circuit.

b) A circuit in which all the components are connected one after the other in a single loop is called a .... circuit.

2 Which of the following statements best describes the current in a parallel circuit? Tick the correct option.

- **A** The total current is the product of the current through the separate components ☐
- **B** The same current flows through each component ☐
- **C** The current decreases each time it passes through a component ☐
- **D** The total current is equal to the sum of the currents through the separate components ☐

3 Which of the following statements best describes what happens to the potential difference in a series circuit? Tick the correct option.

- **A** The potential difference across each component is the same ☐
- **B** The potential difference is divided up between the components ☐
- **C** The potential difference increases as more components are added ☐
- **D** The potential difference is equal to the current ☐

4 The diagram shows a parallel circuit. Each cell provides a potential difference of 1.5V.

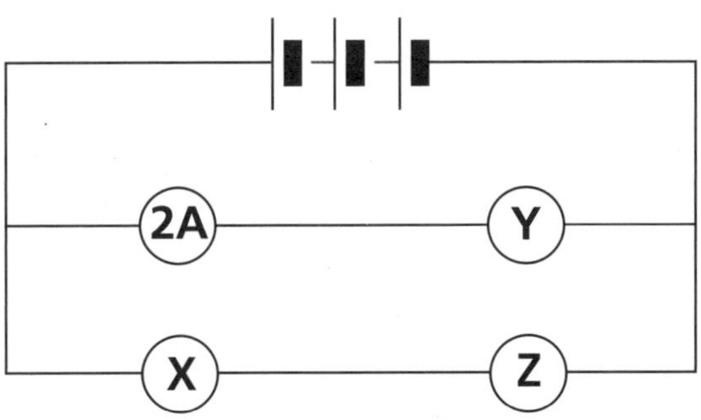

a) What is the value of the current at point X?

....

b) What is the value of the potential difference at point Y?

....

c) What is the value of the potential difference at point Z?

....

Connecting Cells in Series

5 Circle the correct option in the following sentence.

Four 1.5V cells are connected in series, creating a total potential difference of **1.5V / 3V / 5.5V / 6V**.

Currents

Currents

1 Circle the correct option in the following sentence.

The approximate voltage of UK mains electricity is **100V / 230V / 60V / 550V**.

2 Fill in the missing words to complete the following sentences.

a) An .... circuit changes the direction of current flow back and forth continuously. A .... current flows in the same direction.

b) Briefly explain what the 'frequency' of a current is.

....

....

The Three-Pin Plug

3 The diagram below shows a three-pin plug.

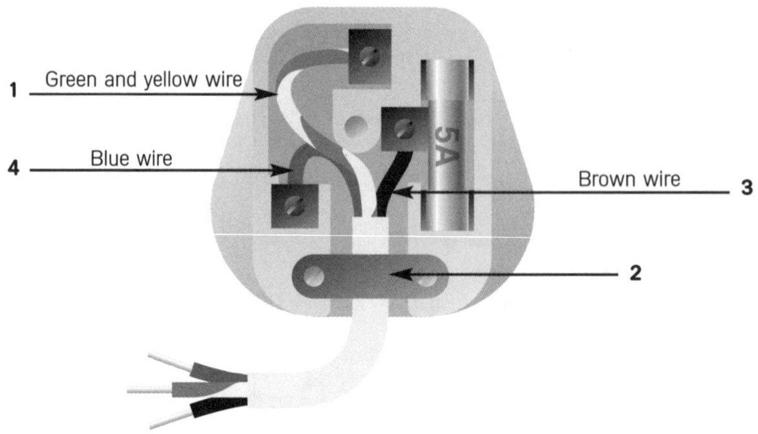

Match statements **A**, **B**, **C** and **D** with the labels **1–4** on the diagram. Write the appropriate numbers in the boxes provided.

A Cable grip ☐

B Earth wire ☐

C Neutral wire ☐

D Live wire ☐

4 What material is used to make the pins of a plug? Briefly explain why it's used.

....

Circuit Breakers and Fuses

Circuit Breakers and Fuses

1 What is the purpose of a circuit breaker or fuse?

2 What is one advantage of circuit breakers over conventional fuses? Tick the correct option.

- **A** They can be reset ☐
- **B** They last longer than fuses ☐
- **C** They are cheaper than fuses ☐
- **D** They are more reliable than fuses ☐

3 Briefly explain how a fuse works.

Earthing

4 The steps **A**, **B**, **C**, **D** and **E** describe how a fuse protects a poorly wired appliance from damage. They are in the wrong order. Number the steps **1–5** to show the correct order.

- **A** Large current flows to earth ☐
- **B** Live wire touches earthed metal casing ☐
- **C** Live current falls to zero ☐
- **D** Current in live wire increases ☐
- **E** Fuse melts ☐

5 What two things protect the appliance and user? Tick the **two** correct options.

- **A** The plug ☐
- **B** The earth wire ☐
- **C** The cabling ☐
- **D** The fuse ☐

Power

Power

1 Which two sets of measurements could you use to calculate the power of an appliance? Tick the **two** correct options.

- **A** Potential difference and time ☐
- **B** Energy transformed and time ☐
- **C** Energy transformed and current ☐
- **D** Potential difference and current ☐
- **E** Current and time ☐
- **F** Charge and time ☐

2 An electric motor works at a current of 3A and a potential difference of 24V. What is the power of the motor?

....

HT Charge

3 **a)** Circle the correct option in the following sentence.

The unit of charge is the **joule / volt / ampere / coulomb**.

b) A 0.5 amp circuit is switched on for 60 seconds. What is the charge?

....

Transforming Energy

4 A simple series circuit contains a switch, a lamp and an ammeter. There is a 6V power supply. When the lamp is switched on for 5 minutes the reading on the ammeter is 3A.

Fill in the missing values to complete the following sentences. Don't forget to specify the units of measure.

a) The charge that flows through the circuit is ....

b) The power of the lamp is ....

c) The energy transformed is ....

5 Fill in the missing word to complete the following sentence.

The .... the potential difference, the more energy transformed per coulomb.

Atoms

1 Which of the following particles can't be found in an atom? Tick the correct option.

- **A** Proton ☐
- **B** Neutron ☐
- **C** Ion ☐
- **D** Electron ☐

2 Explain why an atom as a whole doesn't have an electrical charge.

....

3 What are isotopes?

....

Radioactive Decay

4 Which of the following statements about radioactivity are true? Tick the **three** correct options.

- **A** Radioactive materials have unstable nuclei ☐
- **B** Alpha radiation is a form of radioactive decay ☐
- **C** Radioactive materials become more radioactive as time passes ☐
- **D** Radioactive atoms have stable nuclei ☐
- **E** A gamma particle is a fast-moving electron ☐
- **F** Radioactive isotopes may disintegrate and emit radiation ☐

Alpha Decay

5 **a)** Fill in the missing word to complete the following sentence.

An alpha particle can also be described as a(n) ....

b) An alpha particle is made up of four smaller particles. What are these four particles? Tick the correct option.

- **A** Three protons and one neutron ☐
- **B** Four protons ☐
- **C** Two protons and two electrons ☐
- **D** Two protons and two neutrons ☐

Radiation

Beta Decay

1. Which of the following statements about beta decay are true? Tick the **three** correct options.

   A A beta particle is like an alpha particle ☐

   B A beta particle is a helium nucleus ☐

   C A beta particle is formed when a neutron decays into a proton and an electron ☐

   D When a beta particle is emitted a new element is formed ☐

   E A beta particle is a high-energy electron ☐

Ionisation

2. Fill in the missing words to complete the following sentences.

   a) .... particles can collide with atoms or molecules that are ....

   b) Electrons are knocked out of their structure, and they form .... particles.

   These particles are called ....

3. Give two types of ionising radiation.

   a) ....

   b) ....

Background Radiation

4. Give four sources of background radiation.

   a) ....

   b) ....

   c) ....

   d) ....

5. Explain why background radiation is not harmful to our health.

   ....

Nuclear Fusion and Fission

Nuclear Fusion

1 Nuclear fusion is a self-sustaining reaction. What does this mean? Tick the correct option.

- **A** The fusion reaction is reversible and forms a continuous cycle ☐
- **B** The energy produced by fusion drives further fusion reactions ☐
- **C** The products of one reaction are the reactants for the next ☐
- **D** The reaction always takes place within a closed system ☐

2 Give two examples of nuclear fusion.

a) .... **b)** ....

Nuclear Fission

3 Name the two substances most commonly used for nuclear fission.

a) .... **b)** ....

Nuclear Fission on a Small Scale

4 The diagram illustrates nuclear fission on a small scale.

Match statements **A**, **B**, **C** and **D**, with the labels **1**–**4** on the diagram. Write the appropriate numbers in the boxes provided.

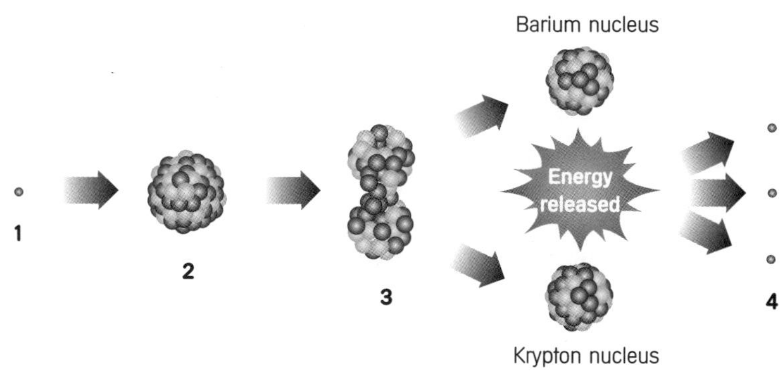

- **A** More neutrons ☐
- **B** Uranium nucleus ☐
- **C** Neutron ☐
- **D** Fission occurs ☐

Nuclear Fission on a Large Scale

5 Which of the following statements about uranium fission are true? Tick the **two** correct options.

- **A** Energy is released in the form of heat ☐
- **B** Heat energy is taken in ☐
- **C** Each reaction releases a huge amount of energy ☐
- **D** Each reaction releases a small amount of energy ☐

Moments

Moments

1 Fill in the missing word to complete the following sentence.

Forces can be used to turn objects about a ....

2 What is a moment?

....

3 What unit is a moment measured in? Tick the correct option.

- **A** Newton (N) ☐
- **B** Kilogram (kg) ☐
- **C** Newton metre (Nm) ☐
- **D** Newtons/metre squared (N/m^2) ☐

4 Write down the equation for calculating moments.

....

....

5 Circle the correct options in the following sentence.

You can increase a moment by **increasing / decreasing** the force applied and **increasing / decreasing** the perpendicular distance between the line of action of the force and the pivot.

Centre of Mass

6 Where is the centre of mass of a symmetrical object found? Tick the correct option.

- **A** Along the axis of symmetry ☐
- **B** Along the edge of the object ☐
- **C** At the point where forces always act ☐
- **D** At the corner of the object ☐

Finding the Centre of Mass

7 Fill in the missing words to complete the following sentence.

A suspended object will always come to rest with its centre of mass directly below the

.... of ....

HT Law of Moments

1. What does the Law of Moments describe?

2. In this diagram, a plank of wood is pivoted at its centre of mass. It has balanced forces. Calculate F_2.

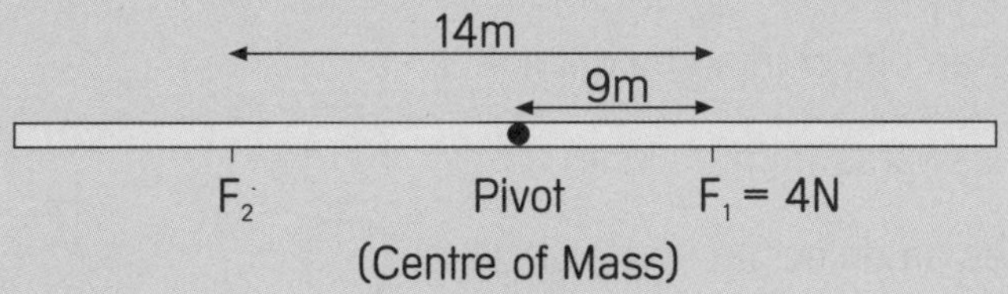

Stability

3. How can the stability of a car be increased? Tick the **two** correct options.

   A By having a higher centre of mass ☐
   B By having a lower centre of mass ☐
   C By having a wider centre of mass ☐
   D By having a wider wheel base ☐
   E By having a narrower wheel base ☐
   F By having a higher wheel base ☐

4. Circle the correct options in the following sentences.

   When an object is tipped it will become unstable when its centre of mass is **directly / just / not** above its base. This is because the action of its weight creates a **force / moment / pull** that causes it to continue turning.

5. A box is tipped so that its centre of mass is just outside the base. Which of the following sentences best describes what happens when the hand holding it is removed? Tick the correct option.

   A The box rocks backwards and forwards ☐
   B The box wobbles for a few minutes ☐
   C The box remains balanced on its edge ☐
   D The box falls ☐

Centripetal Force and Gravity

Motion in a Circle

1 Give two examples of objects that move in circular, or near circular, paths.

a) ....

b) ....

Centripetal Force

2 Which of the following sentences best describes a centripetal force? Tick the correct option.

A A force that keeps an object in a straight line ☐

B A force that acts outwards from a circle ☐

C A force that pushes an object around a circle ☐

D A force that acts towards the centre of a circle ☐

3 **a)** An athlete throwing the hammer swings the ball and chain around in a circle several times before letting go. What force keeps the ball travelling in the circular path? Tick the correct option.

A Friction ☐ **B** Gravity ☐

C Tension ☐ **D** Magnetism ☐

b) A car travels at a constant speed around a circular race track. What force keeps the car travelling in the circle? Tick the correct option.

A Friction ☐ **B** Gravity ☐

C Tension ☐ **D** Magnetism ☐

4 List two ways in which centripetal force can be increased.

a) ....

b) ....

Gravity and our Solar System

5 **a)** What shape is the orbit of a planet? Tick the correct option.

A A circle ☐ **B** An ellipse ☐

C A square ☐ **D** An oblong ☐

b) What is the name of the force that holds a planet in its orbit? Tick the correct option.

A Magnetism ☐ **B** Friction ☐

C Tension ☐ **D** Gravity ☐

Centripetal Force and Gravity

Gravity and Orbiting Speed

1 Circle the correct options in the following sentences.

a) Moving a planet further away from a star **reduces / increases** the force of gravity between them.

b) The further away from a star a planet is, the **more / less** time it takes the planet to orbit the star.

Artificial Satellites

2 a) How long is the orbital period of a geostationary satellite? Tick the correct option.

- **A** 6 hours ☐
- **B** 12 hours ☐
- **C** 24 hours ☐
- **D** 48 hours ☐

b) Are the following sentences **true** or **false**?

i) Geostationary satellites stay at the same point above the equator. ....

ii) Geostationary satellites move around the Earth at a different rate than the Earth spins.

....

iii) Geostationary satellites scan the Earth from a much closer range than a polar orbiting satellite.

....

3 a) Which of the following is a polar orbiting satellite most likely to be used for? Tick the correct option.

- **A** A space telescope ☐
- **B** Satellite television ☐
- **C** Monitoring Arctic weather systems ☐
- **D** Telephone communications ☐

b) A polar orbiting satellite is much closer to the Earth than a geostationary satellite. How does this affect its orbit time? Explain your answer.

....

....

Reflection and Refraction

Reflection of Light

1 This diagram shows light reflecting off a plane mirror.

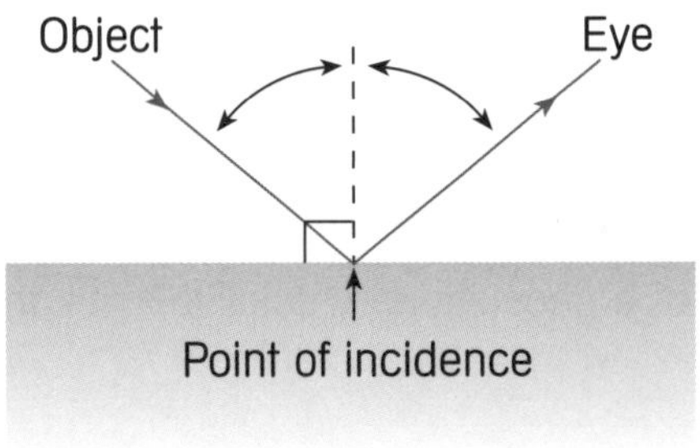

a) What name is given to the dotted line marked on the diagram? Tick the correct option.

A Incident ray ▢ **B** Normal ▢

C Reflected ray ▢ **D** Refracted ray ▢

b) Fill in the missing words to complete the following sentences.

i) The ray which travels away from the mirror and into the eye is called the

.... ray.

ii) The angle of reflection is equal to the angle of ....

Refraction of Light

2 a) A ray of light enters a glass block at an angle of 82°. What happens to the ray of light as it travels from air into glass? Tick the correct option.

A It speeds up ▢

B It continues in the same direction ▢

C It speeds up and is refracted away from the normal ▢

D It slows down and is refracted towards the normal ▢

b) Which of the following statements about refraction is true? Tick the correct option.

A The angle of incidence is always bigger than the angle of refraction ▢

B The angle of incidence is always smaller than the angle of refraction ▢

C Refraction occurs when light crosses the interface of two media with different optical densities ▢

D Refraction only occurs between glass and air ▢

Images Produced by Mirrors

1 a) What word is used to describe an image that is upside down when compared to the object?

....

b) What word is used to describe an image where the rays of light appear to come directly from the image?

....

2 a) Describe a concave mirror in terms of its curvature.

....

b) Describe a convex mirror in terms of its curvature.

....

3 What is the point called where all the rays of light converge?

....

4 Circle the correct options in the following sentences.

a) A convex mirror forms an image that is **smaller / bigger** than the object. The image is **real / virtual** and **upright / inverted**.

b) A concave mirror forms an image inside its curve at the point where all the rays of light **converge / separate**.

5 a) If an object is placed closer to the mirror than the focal point, how is the observed image described? Tick the correct option.

A Virtual, upright, enlarged ☐

B Real, upright, enlarged ☐

C Virtual, upright, smaller ☐

D Real, inverted, smaller ☐

b) If an object is placed further away from a concave mirror than the focal point, how is the observed image described? Tick the correct option.

A Virtual, upright, enlarged ☐

B Real, upright, enlarged ☐

C Virtual, upright, smaller ☐

D Real, inverted, smaller ☐

Lenses

Images Produced by Lenses

1 Fill in the missing words to complete the following sentences.

a) A lens is a piece of transparent material that .... light rays.

b) There are two types of lens: the diverging, or ...., lens, and the converging, or

...., lens.

Diverging and Converging Lenses

2 What type of image is produced by a diverging lens? Tick the correct option.

A Virtual and upright ☐

B Virtual and inwards ☐

C Virtual and enlarged ☐

D Virtual and inverted ☐

3 Complete the diagram to show what happens to rays of light when they pass through a converging lens.

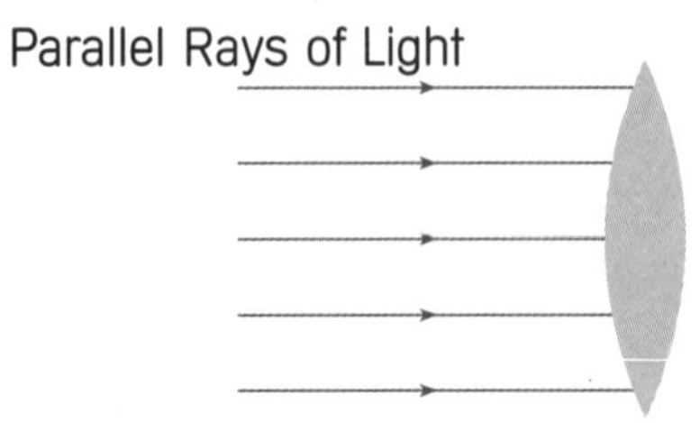

The Camera

4 **a)** What kind of lens is used in a camera? Tick the correct option.

A Diverging lens ☐

B Concave lens ☐

C Pinhole lens ☐

D Converging lens ☐

b) Fill in the missing words to complete the following sentence.

The type of lens used in a camera means that the image formed on the film is

.... and .... to the lens than the actual object. ☐

Sound Waves

1 Which of the following sentences about sound is true? Tick the correct option.

- **A** Sound travels faster than light
- **B** Sound will travel in a vacuum
- **C** Sound travels as a wave
- **D** Sound will not travel in a solid

2 What does the quality of a note depend on?

....

3 How is an echo produced? Tick the correct option.

- **A** Reflected sound waves
- **B** Refracted sound waves
- **C** Diffracted sound waves
- **D** Dispersed sound waves

Frequency and Pitch

4 **a)** What unit is frequency measured in? Tick the correct option.

- **A** Metres
- **B** Metres per second
- **C** Hertz
- **D** Watts

b) Fill in the missing words to complete the following sentences.

The frequency of a sound wave affects the .... As the frequency is increased,

the .... of the sound becomes ....

Amplitude and Loudness

5 Which of the following sentences about the amplitude of sound is true? Tick the correct option.

- **A** The loudness is affected by the amplitude
- **B** The pitch is affected by the amplitude
- **C** The wavelength depends on the amplitude
- **D** The speed depends on the amplitude

6 What happens to the sound as the amplitude is increased?

....

Ultrasound

Ultrasound

1. What is ultrasound? Tick the correct option.

   A Sound with a wavelength so low that people can't hear it ☐

   B Sound with a wavelength so high that people can't hear it ☐

   C Sound with a frequency so high that people can't hear it ☐

   D Sound with a frequency so low that people can't hear it ☐

2. What frequencies are counted as ultrasound? Tick the correct option.

   A Less than 20 000Hz ☐ **B** 20Hz to 20kHz ☐

   C Greater than 20 000Hz ☐ **D** Greater than 40 000Hz ☐

3. Fill in the missing words to complete the following sentence.

   As ultrasonic waves pass from one medium into another, they are partially .... at the ....

Uses of Ultrasound

4. Why is ultrasound used for pre-natal scans, instead of X-rays? Tick the **two** correct options.

   A X-rays can't produce images of the baby ☐

   B X-rays could harm the baby ☐

   C X-rays could harm the mother ☐

   D X-rays don't produce clear pictures ☐

5. When used for flaw detection, what happens to some of the ultrasonic waves when they hit a flaw? Tick the correct option.

   A They are diffracted ☐ **B** They are refracted ☐

   C They are absorbed ☐ **D** They are reflected ☐

6. **a)** How do ultrasound waves clean the surface of an object that is suspended in liquid?

   ....

   b) Give two advantages of using ultrasound for cleaning delicate objects.

   i) ....

   ii) ....

The Motor Effect

1. Fill in the missing word to complete the following sentence.

   The motor effect uses current to produce ....

2. What happens when there is a current flowing through a magnetic field? Tick the correct option.

   A Nothing

   B The conductor moves

   C The two cancel each other out

   D The magnetic field disappears

3. Give two ways in which the size of the force on the wire can be increased.

   a) ....

   b) ....

4. Give two ways in which the direction of the force on the wire can be reversed.

   a) ....

   b) ....

Direct Current Motor

5. What kind of motors used in a range of household appliances use the principle of the motor effect?

   ....

6. Fill in the missing words to complete the following sentences.

   a) As a current flows through the coil, a magnetic field is formed around the coil. This creates an

   ....

   b) The magnetic field interacts with the permanent magnetic field which exists between the two

   ...., North and South.

   c) A force acts on both sides of the coil, so the coil .... and a simple motor is generated.

Generating Electrical Current

Electromagnetic Induction

1 a) Fill in the missing words to complete the following sentence.

Electromagnetic induction uses .... to produce a ....

b) What do generators produce using electromagnetic induction?

....

2 Circle the correct options in the following sentences.

a) If a wire cuts through the lines of force of a magnetic field, a potential difference is **induced / stopped** between the ends of the wire.

b) If the wire is part of a **partial / complete** circuit, a current will be induced.

3 Moving the magnet into the coil induces a current in one direction. In what two ways can a current be induced in the opposite direction?

a) ....

b) ....

4 What happens if there's no movement of magnet or coil?

....

Increasing Potential Difference

5 a) Fill in the missing words to complete the following sentences.

i) The size of the induced potential difference can be increased by increasing the

.... of the coil.

ii) Potential difference can also be increased by increasing the .... of movement of the magnet or the coil.

b) Give two other methods that can be used to increase the potential difference.

i) ....

ii) ....

Transformers

1 What does a transformer do?

....

....

2 **a)** Fill in the missing words to complete the following sentence.

Transformers are made of two coils: the .... and ....

coils. These coils are wrapped around a soft .... core.

b) **i)** Which coil creates the output?

....

ii) Which coil creates the input?

....

3 Fill in the missing word to complete the following sentence.

An .... current creates a continually changing magnetic field in the core.

Step-Up and Step-Down Transformers

4 Circle the correct words in the following sentences.

a) In a step-up transformer, the potential difference across the secondary coil is **greater / less** than the potential difference across the primary coil.

b) In a step-down transformer, the potential difference across the secondary coil is **greater / less** than the potential difference across the primary coil.

5 Fill in the missing words to complete the following sentence.

Step-up and step-down transformers are used in the ....

to ensure the efficient .... of electricity.

6 What type of transformer is used when electricity is transferred from a power station to power lines?

....

Stars

Formation of Stars

1. During the early stages of star formation, what is created as clouds of dust and gas are pulled together by gravity? Tick the correct option.

   A Heat ☐
   B Black holes ☐
   C Comets ☐
   D Gravity ☐

2. Circle the correct options in the following sentences.

   a) When the mass becomes hot enough, hydrogen fuses to form **nitrogen / helium / oxygen / phosphorus**.

   b) This nuclear fusion releases **dust / energy / nothing / clouds** and produces all naturally occurring **elements / stones / radiation / water**.

3. How old is the Sun believed to be?

   ....

Our Galaxy and the Universe

4. Draw lines between the boxes to match each object to its description.

Object	Description
Sun	Galaxy
Milky Way	Planet
Jupiter	Star

5. How many stars are there in the Milky Way? Tick the correct option.

   A Hundreds ☐ **B** Thousands ☐
   C Millions ☐ **D** Billions ☐

The Life Cycle of a Star

6. Fill in the missing words to complete the following sentence.

   The star will stay the same size if the .... pressure and .... are equal.

Smaller Stars

1 a) What will our Sun expand to become? Tick the correct option.

A White dwarf ☐ B Red giant ☐

C Neutron star ☐ D Supernova ☐

b) What happens after this?

....

....

Bigger Stars

2 Stars which are at least four times the size of the Sun expand to become another type of star. What type of star do they become? Tick the correct option.

A Neutron star ☐ B Black hole ☐

C Red giant ☐ D Red supergiant ☐

3 What is a supernova? Tick the correct option.

A A large star ☐ B An exploding star ☐

C Two stars colliding ☐ D The final stage in a star's life cycle ☐

4 Circle the correct options in the following sentences.

a) After becoming a supernova, a star that is ten times bigger than the Sun will form a **black hole / neutron star / white dwarf / red giant**.

b) After becoming a supernova, a star that is more than ten times the size of the Sun will leave behind a **black hole / neutron star / white dwarf / red giant**.

HT Recycling Stellar Material

5 a) Which element do stars need in order to undergo nuclear fusion?

....

b) As a star explodes, its elements are distributed throughout the Universe. Name two forms in which these elements can be recycled.

i) ....

ii) ....

Notes